How to
Get Over It!
in
30 Days!

Daily Inspirations for when you hit Rock Bottom

Adair f. White-johnson, Ph.D.

The Empowerment House & Johnson Tribe Publishing

10/27/13

Carol,

Be Inspired!!

Published by
Johnson Tribe Publishing, LLC
Atlanta, GA

Johnson Tribe Publishing materials may be purchased for education, business, or promotional use. Author is also available for speaking engagements. For information please contact us at (888) 400-7302, email us at or visit us at

Manufactured in the United States of America

10 9 8 7 6 5 4 3 2 1

FIRST EDITION – August 2013

Creative Direction: Adair F. White-johnson, Ph.D.
Edited by: Amanda J. Perkins, Soulful Storytellers, Inc.
Graphic Design: DzineBK, LLC
Book Design: Adair F. White-Johnson, Ph.D.
Book Consultation: The Bestsellers Project

Library of Congress Catalog Card Number:

ISBN 13: 978-0-9896733-4-1
ISBN 10: 0989673340

DEDICATION

This is dedicated to my children, Susan, Najja, Jaja, Taji and Zuri who inspire me to *Get Over It!* every day…

Introduction

How to "Get Over It!" in 30 Days

"Get Over It!" means to just let things go that do not serve a positive purpose in your life. It means that you should do everything from the core of your existence… not holding back and sucking in the final morsel of air to exhale confidently. You learn from your mistakes and use those mistakes as starting points towards change. Never embracing failure but knowing when to accept defeat. Understanding what makes you weaker but focusing on what makes you stronger. It means that you love hard, play hard, work hard, Mommy hard, Daddy hard, wife hard, husband hard, sister hard, brother hard and friend hard! You never skimp on challenges because you have invested your total self. This is the only way you can get over and get through things to keep it moving…the only way that you can bounce back after hitting rock

bottom. This coupled with the strength and the faith that comes from your belief and commitment to a higher power can only empower you. And for me, it means constantly leaning on my shield of faith and understanding that God's plan for me is the only plan that will ultimately prevail. The inspirational messages in this book are designed to empower you to make decisions that will lead you towards emotional prosperity because you deserve to be happy.

Although you may not be "fixed" in 30 days after reading this book, you will be able to think about your life in a different way. That is my primary intent and each day provides a message that will inspire and empower your thought process. It also includes action steps and affirmations to help you begin to change the way you think so eventually you can change the way you behave...Remember, it all begins with your mindset.

Twelve Tricks to Get Over It!

You have to exercise your mind effectively because your brain power always serves as the impetus to move toward change. I believe that there are basically twelve "tricks" to learning how to *Get Over It!* and how to think positive, live positive and make positive choices…

1.   When something is itching, scratch it. If you don't, it will keep itching. Don't ignore the things that cause you pain. If you do it will continue hurting even if you mask the pain.

2.   Don't just buy things just because they "look good." Make sure they are good for you. Remember that everything that looks good on the surface doesn't necessarily look good in your life. Always imagine yourself and your life in a situation before you just jump into it because it "looks good."

3.   Just because you can't sing doesn't mean that you should only hum. You may not be the next

Beyoncé or Usher but never deny yourself the opportunity to enjoy things! You can enjoy doing something without having an ulterior motive.

4.   Remember that a bucket can be filled one drop at a time so you don't have to fill it in one shot. You can reach your own ladder of success by climbing one rung at a time...you don't have to race to the top just to get there. And remember that the small things eventually build up to the bigger things in life.

5.   Dreams don't come with a warranty or a guarantee. It's your job to ensure that they are never broken.

6.   One man's junk may be another man's treasure but you don't have to accept it. Never accept anything secondhand unless you want to because you are not a secondhand person. But if you decide you want to accept it then make sure it is worthy of you...

7.   Know the difference between courage and courageous. We are all born with courage but it's

when we use it at the right time that makes us "courageous."

8.   Spiritual, emotional and mental paralysis can have a worst impact than physical paralysis. If you don't feel anything in your heart, your soul and you don't use your brain then you have paralyzed your ability to live a worthwhile life. At least with physical paralysis you can still live a fulfilling life...I'm not convinced that you can do so if you are living with spiritual, emotional and mental paralysis.

9.   You own the power of change. So change it.

10.   Life isn't fair. But so what? What are you going to do about it?

11.   Bringing volume to your silenced voice doesn't mean you have to shout! Instead, it means you may have to adjust the sound on someone else's speakers.

12.   Don't leave without your bag. Make sure that after the end of every relationship you fill your bag with knowledge and lessons so that you can grow

from the experience. Your bag should be filled with what you need to learn and grow from the relationship...the good, the bad and the ugly.

Day 1

"Opposites Attract"

Without fear there is no courage.

Without sadness there is no joy.

Without pain there is no pleasure.

Without hate there is no love.

Without conflict there is no peace.

Without enemies there are no friends.

Without struggle there is no significance.

Without sin there is no forgiveness.

Without inequity there is no justice.

Without mental enslavement there is no

intellectual empowerment.

Without weakness there is no strength.

Without loss, there is no gain.

Without questions there are no answers.

Without negative signs there are no positive signs.

Without death there is no life.

Without choices there are no decisions.

And without hope there are no dreams.

LESSON:

Life is full of experiences, emotions and "things" that are two sides of the same coin. The two "go together, fit together and heighten each other. Each contributing to the ultimate bliss." Sometimes you face the "worst" in your life before the "better" emerges along your path. But know that it is coming because your life is abundant with polar opposites and you are competent and blessed to own the power in order to balance your own scales...Weigh yourself carefully.

ACTION:

Take out a plain sheet of paper and draw a line down the middle of it. Review five lines of the poem and try to remember any experiences that you may have had. Think about the worst of the situation and then write down the best of the situation. This can be a first step to Get Over It!

Day 2

"More is Less"

Sometimes "more" is actually "less."

The more you have, the less you want or need.

Let me explain:

You see, the more that you have of God in your life is the less time you have to deal with the devil.

The more faith you fill your spirit with is the less self-doubt that you feel daily.

The more love that is in your heart is the less hatred that flows through your bloodstream.

The more dreams you have leads to less nightmares of what your future will be.

The more clarity you have on your goals is the less confusion you'll have about your purpose in life.

The more positives you attract in your world is the less negative energy that will gravitate towards you.

And the more you keep open, honest, inspiring people around you, the less "drama" will come into your life.

The more self-empowered you become is the less likely you are to give up on yourself.

The more goals you achieve are likely to be the less failures on your list.

The more you give is the less you have and the less you probably need anyway.

The more you become that man/woman of your word then the less folks will question your integrity.

The more you love yourself, the less you will depend on others loving you the wrong way.

The more self-esteem you build, the less opportunity others have to tear you down.

Oh yeah, the more beautiful you are inside then the less ugly you will allow others to make you feel.

The more you allow yourself to trust and believe in the steps that God has ordered for you is the less you'll have to ask about the path that he has chosen for you to follow.

You see, we are already "so much" but we are destined to be "so much more."

And that's okay if it uplifts and strengthens your life...

More faith, more positivity, more love, more confidence, more assurance, more empowerment...

Ah yes, "more" of the right stuff is "less" of the wrong crap... More is less.

LESSON:

Fill your life with "more" of the things that will empower you... It's the only way to guarantee that your weaknesses will be "less."

AFFIRMATION:

"I got MORE but I may need LESS!"

Day 3

"The SWOT of Me"

Sometimes we look in the mirror and we don't recognize the person staring back at us...Sort of like a reflection of a person who never really was.

And there are times in our lives when we "lose" ourselves and forget our self-worth because we are caught up living another life that really doesn't define us.

It may be those times when we are actually chasing rainbows that don't have pots of gold at the end of them that we realize that it was just "fool's gold" all along...

Perhaps it is at those moments that we need to evaluate our lives to determine what our strengths, weaknesses, opportunities and threats are.

Strengths focuses on what we are good at and the good things in our lives...those things that can inspire us and keep us dreaming and knowing that

"Yes, we can!" These are the characteristics/things in our lives that can place us at an advantage over us to help others to achieve our goals.

Weaknesses are the exact opposite of our strengths because these are the characteristics/things that slow our growth and development. These qualities/obstacles or stumbling blocks can prohibit us from developing into positive beings and submerges our productive thoughts and activities under a concrete slab of negativity. What type of waste is in your life now? What are your weaknesses that you are aware of? Who are the "weak" people that you allow to remain in your life? What are your consistent weak moments?

Opportunities focus on those external chances that you may receive to make a positive difference in your life. How many times have you passed on an opportunity because of doubt or fear? I think we miss good opportunities in our lifetimes because we have a fear of the unknown and the fear of failure. We would rather live in a "comfortable hell" (as my friend Tre says) than reach out and take a chance in an "uncomfortable heaven." We often get too comfortable in our skin and our environments that we live in a victim's mentality and will not seize the opportunity to move toward positive change in our lives. If you are going to *Get Over It!* then you have to take advantage of some of the opportunities that may come your way. You see, there will be people who offer you a chance but it is your responsibility to accept the opportunity. That's what opportunity is all about.

God can definitely bless you with talent but if you don't take the opportunity to "grow" the talent then it is basically a talent wasted. As you continue to work on your self-directed search, don't forget to take advantage of some opportunities along the way.

Threats...Be wary of these because they represent those challenges to your opportunities, dreams and to your sanity. These are the external elements that can threaten your progress and seek to destroy your dreams. You need to be prepared at all times for those elements and those people who only wish the worst for you.

Be wary of yourself too, sometimes we can be our own worst enemy because we live in that comfortable hell and will threaten our own reality... So as we stare in that mirror and gaze into those eyes and we are struggling to get a glimpse of that soul inside, we need to remove those layers of pain, lift the veil of heartache so there is nothing left to hide. We don't need to focus on what "coulda, woulda, shoulda" been but simply wasn't... But we can begin to accept and work on what really is. So who is that person staring at us, who could it be? Those eyes look like mine but is it really ME?

LESSON:

"To Thine Own Self Be True"

ACTION:

Complete your own SWOT analysis of your life. Make a list of your strengths, weaknesses, opportunities and threats in your life. This is one of the first steps to move towards change.

Shakespeare, http://www.enotes.com/hamlet-text/act-i-scene-iii#ham-1-3-82)

Day 4

"I'm Not Gon' Hurt Anymore"

If someone is hurting you then why do you want them in your life?

If someone is abusing you then why would you need them in your life?

If someone is consistently lying to you then what is the purpose of them in your life?

Hmmmm....

These are questions that you have to answer from deep within yourself. You have to dig deep, face the truth and deal with the issues within yourself that allow you to accept these people in your life.

I don't think that we intentionally place a "welcome mat" at the front door of our lives to invite negativity in. But some of us become that "provocative victim" where we play games and start things that we have no intention of finishing and we build relationships that we knew were unhealthy from the start and then we wonder "what happened?"

We see the signs way ahead that direct us to make the right turn out of the relationship but yet we still drive straight ahead into the abusive and negative situation because we are searching for a love/relationship that may never exist with this person. Or, we keep trying to "change" that family member because we think they are supposed to love us in a certain way just because "we are family." And then we are the ones hurt. We feel betrayed. We feel lost. And we feel confused.

You see, most relationships make you feel that way sometimes anyway but it's when it becomes consistently unhealthy that we must learn to just walk away. We must learn that when it's time to go...It's just time to go. Whether it's the relationships we have with our significant others, family, friends or even supervisors. If it hurts us worse than it soothes us then we have to question why we really need it in our lives.

Sometimes people love us the best the way they know how and then we try to change that love and train that love in order to breed a new love. But that just doesn't work either. We can't control how people love us...just how we accept that love. You own the power of change so you can change who you let love you... And if it hurts real badly, just let it go. Take yourself through the mourning and healing process of letting them go out of your life.... Love them differently now...Or don't love them at all. Love yourself more and know when you've had enough. Yes, hurt hurts...That's what it is supposed to do. But letting go releases "stuff" and that's what it is supposed to do...

So let go of the hurt, lies, and emotional, psychological and/or physical abuse that may encircle a relationship that you are in. Let go of that negative relationship you may have with your own self because sometimes we hurt ourselves more than anyone else is capable of... I could go on and on but it's simple...Know when it is time to "walk away." And know when it is time to *"Let go and Let God."*

LESSON:

Examine the relationships in your life and own that power of change to determine which relationship you need to walk away from.

AFFIRMATION:

"I can let anyone GO from my life that consistently hurts me!"

Day 5

"You don't own ME"

Letter to **YOU**:

You can't steal my joy because you didn't
put it there.

And you can't ask me to return my
happiness because I didn't get it from you.

You see, my purpose is not defined by your
existence and my emotional sobriety is not
dependent upon your approval.

I am independent, free-spirited, priceless
and honest.

And you can't hold me back.

My dreams are bigger than your negative
reality.

And my faith is stronger than your spiteful
words.

My spirit is full of inspiration

And my soul has already been committed to
excellence.

So you can't touch this.

I already know that I am "so much" but I've also learned that I can be "so much" more. With or without your support.

The key is to hold on to my own positive energy, to never limit my possibilities, to never allow my disabilities to disable my abilities and to keep on dreaming.

See I know that when I finish one dream I've got to start working on the next one.

And when I'm walking on a lonely road that may be less travelled then it is actually okay. Because God is actually right by my side.

And he supports me.

So my friend, if you can't be there for me, with me and next to me then you can't be near me.

My life is too precious to waste on your negativity.

I won't allow you to steal things that you never gave to me in the first place...my hopes, my dreams, my faith, my spirit, my heart, my soul, my gifts, my talents, my determination, my happiness, my .....
You can't have them because they just don't belong to you.
I am. I can. I will. I do.
And it's because of who I am and not because of you.
Thanks be to God.

LESSON:

If "they" cannot support you then what purpose do they serve in your life? If they have no purpose then they should have no space...It's time to "let go" of some people in your life who only bring negative energy and strife...

ACTION:

Make a list of 3 things that you think were "stolen" from you in your life. Then, determine if you can get them back. If you can't then Get Over It! If you think you can get them back write down 3 thoughts about how to get them back.

Day 6

"I feel him all over me"

When God is on your mind then your thoughts are empowered, enriched, exceptional and engaging.

When God is in your ear his whispers sound like roars of thunder and you can clearly hear the Word of the Lord.

When God is in your arms you can feel his love wrapped around you to protect you from negativity.

When God is in your feet the road you travel will seem less troublesome and your soles become less weary.

When God is in your heart your heartbeat will be stronger since it is filled with his love...
You'll want to do more, give more, be more and love more.

When God is in your eyes you will see the difference your kindness and generosity make in the world.

When God is in your stomach your life will be nourished with meals of faith and endurance.

When God is in your nose scents of sin and destruction will be apparent so you will recognize the smell of evil.

When God is in your mouth you will taste the sweetness of life and spit out the bitterness of pain and sorrow.

When God is in your body and soul you know it, you breathe it, you feel it, and your spirit shows it....You just have to believe it.

LESSON:

Know your body parts.

AFFIRMATION:

"I know my body, I know my soul and I know how he makes me feel."

Day 7

"Running Around in Circles"

Have you ever seen a dog chase its own tail?

They go around and around and they look pretty crazy huh?

And then we wonder why they do it...

Well, as humans we do the same thing...

We spin ourselves in circles by doing the same wrong things over and over again...

They're called bad habits and we often do them because it's easier...

Easier to live in a "comfortable hell" then to strive for life in an "uncomfortable heaven."

And then we think we are "happy."

Hmmmm... So at what point do we stop and begin to make a change?

To break the cycle of self-destruction and perhaps self-inflicted pain?

What will it take to allow ourselves to let the negativity in our lives and the bad habits go? Hmmmm...

The difference between humans and dogs is that we simply have a greater degree of ownership... We know better so we can do better and we own the power of choice and change to make a difference.

Use it.

LESSON:

Where is your tail? Are you chasing it or, are you in control of it?

ACTION:

List 3 bad habits you have, 3 ways you have tried to break them and 1 new direction that you can take to break them.

Day 8

"Listen"

Don't you absolutely hate when people don't listen to you?

When you feel as though you are talking to a wall because no one is responding to your words? How frustrating is that?

Well, how do you think God feels when you do not listen to his words in your spirit?

When you fail to follow the dreams that he has implanted in your heart?

When you ignore the "signs," the "feelings" and the "opportunities" that are placed before you? We are often guilty when we stagnate our hopes and abbreviate our goals because we just don't listen to what our spirit tells us.

We limit our possibilities by doubting our abilities.

We fear what we want most and embrace what we need least.

We settle for less and we accept the least. And then we think we are happy with the results. That is definitely not the plan that God has for us. There is an abundance of joy and happiness in the universe and you deserve as piece of it but you have to listen to the voice that God has instilled in you.

Don't question his plans for you. Don't question your purpose that he has created for you. What's for you is for you.

Your life was designed for greatness but you first have to listen.

You have to feel what God has placed in your soul to understand your direction that will lead to your destiny.

God's words should not fall upon deaf ears because the "sound" of his voice should resonate in your spirit and order your steps.

It all begins with faith.

I've said this before…you need your faith in order to listen and trust in God. To know that when he speaks to you, he is speaking to you directly and this is the part where you are still to listen.

Hearing his voice in your heart will "free" you to walk down that uncomfortable road to greatness and travel along the road less travelled to self-fulfillment.

Empowering your heart, empowering your soul, empowering your spirit and empowering your dreams all begin with listening to the words that God is speaking to you.

You can't ignore him because God doesn't "go away."

You can't "walk away" from him because God is with you wherever you go. And you can't pretend like he is not there because he is felt everywhere.

Ah yes, we know that when folks don't listen to what we are saying it is very frustrating and at times disappointing.

But yet we want to ignore the words that God speaks to us daily.

Stop it. Just stop it.

He knows and he lets YOU know that the dreams in your soul are there for YOU.

Listen and follow your dreams...

Empower your dreams. Empower yourself with the knowledge that God is always on your side...

He supports you and he believes in you and what you can do. He has given you those dreams to make your reality.

And when you finish with one dream he always has another for you to follow.

Be inspired.

Be empowered.

Be still to listen.

LESSON:

Being ignored is frustrating and we often think it doesn't make sense. We want others to listen to us and follow OUR instructions. Well, in this life you are charged with doing the same thing. Listen to what is in your heart, don't ignore the "signs" and follow the "drive" in your soul to achieve all of your goals. After all, it is God speaking to you...and when he speaks, we must all stop to listen.

AFFIRMATION:

"I will be STILL and LISTEN today."

Day 9

"I see you..."

If joy is in your heart then we will see it in your smile.

If love is in your soul then we will feel it in your hugs.

If positivity is in your personality then we will understand it in your actions.

And if God is in your SPIRIT then we will know the "real" you.

LESSON:

Who you really are emerges in everything you do.

ACTION:

Think about the circumstances when you feel the most "real" and genuine. What are 2 of these moments?

Day 10

"It just didn't work out"

Sometimes Life just doesn't work the way we want it to...no matter how hard we try. Sometimes Love just doesn't work the way we want it to...no matter how much we give. Sometimes Friendships just don't work out...no matter how much we trusted in them. Sometimes Jobs just don't last as long as we want and need them to...no matter how much time and energy we put into them.

The loss of Life, Love, Friendships and Jobs can be devastating to our hearts and souls but your commitment and faith to *YOURSELF* should never waver.

You know that God orders your steps and you will follow that rocky path he has set forth for you because you understand that it is really just your stepping stone to greatness. You know you won't let any disabilities disable your abilities.

And you know that you will still smile after any of these losses because you still have Faith and somehow, someway, it will work out.

You own the spirit of positivity and the power of change so you will begin the process of moving forward.
Nothing will stop you.

Yes, "stuff" happens and it hurts real badly but you have the strength and faith in your soul to remain a "believer" and know that your new tomorrow actually begins today.

We all go through "stuff" in our lives and we are not "special" because of it so we shouldn't feel as though we deserve a "pass" in our world because we are "hurting."

Instead, we should stock up on our ammunition so we can come out "shooting" with positive moves each time we are hurting and we can destroy the negativity aimed our way... So, let's start our day by "Getting over it, Getting through it and Keeping it moving."

LESSON:

Get Over It, Get Through It and Keep It Moving....

AFFIRMATION:

"Yes I can Get Over It, Through It and Keep It Moving!"

Day 11

"No Apologies Accepted"

Never apologize for who you are...

Just apologize for what you did.

Say "sorry" when you are wrong but never be a "sorry" person.

Never just dream about what you "want" to do...

Focus on what you "can" and. "will do."

Say that you are a "believer" and then act like you "believe."

Never share that you have a "passion" if it's only for another person and not for your life.

Say "I am. I can. I will. I do." and know that it's not just all because of you.

Thanks be to God.

Never "walk" down a hill if there's another road to follow that leads you to the same place.

Life has many great opportunities.

Never look in the mirror and not recognize who you see...Just a reflection of a person *who never really was.*

Say what you mean but mean what you say...

Just know that just because you "think" it doesn't mean you have to "say" it.

Never limit your possibilities; capabilities and opportunities...

Just keep them endless.

LESSON:

When life "sucks," Just "suck it up" and keep trying.

ACTION:

Write down what your professional and personal possibilities are and then write down what opportunities you may have...Is there a connection?

Day 12

"Just Rub Me the Right Way and I'll Shine"

Sometimes it takes the things that tarnish us to make us ultimately shine.

And the stupidity of our actions that show us some flaws of our brilliant minds.

It takes our selfishness to realize that we should already know how to freely give.

And our insecurities about ourselves that makes us wonder about how to improve ourselves, how we really want to live.

It's the tone in our angry voices that remind us of the things we are passionate about.

And the release of the pain and anger that makes us scream and shout. Knowing the hurt in our hearts reflects how we truly feel.

And sharing our feelings is how we "keep it real."

Betrayal by others leads us to use the forgiveness embedded in our souls

But feeling discouraged about it all should force us to consider taking a different road.

While our disappointment in some actions and results can teach us that we have the resiliency to "bounce back," it's the suffering because of our behavior that pushes us on the "right track."

If our emotional impoverishment reflects what we are really starving for, then the meal planned with positivity and enrichment will feed our spirits more.

Our impatience with God reminds us that yes, we are trying to do the right things but those "things" are just not happening as we want them to,

But leaning on our shields of faith remind us that ultimately he will move those mountains, he will help us, he WILL come through.

So since the failure of plan "a" shows that we can still dream and we create a plan "b,"

We know that we are still working on unlocking ourselves from all of the negative dead weight...on becoming "free."

And yes, all of these negative characteristics may
seem harsh and mean,
But really, they only allow us to become better,
stronger and own the audacity to *STILL* dream.

LESSON:

    *Yes, tarnish, stupidity, selfishness, insecurity,
anger, hurt, betrayal, disappointment,
impoverishment, and impatience can cast
doubting shadows over your life but remember
that opposites attract...and for every heartache,
there is joy and for every prayer there is an
answer.*

AFFIRMATION:

    "Despite and in spite of it all, I still believe."

Day 13

"I Forgive ME First"

Learning how to forgive.

Hmmmm...

Walking that uncomfortable road of forgiveness is not easy but I think that it is necessary and required to be a "true" Christian.

It is the "heart" of what it means to be Christian. This includes forgiving yourself which is sometimes the hardest thing to do. We can't figure out how to forgive ourselves so we turn to God and pray for forgiveness.

We often think that if God can forgive us, then that will empower us to forgive ourselves.

Hmmmm...

It is imperative that you learn to forgive yourself or you won't know how to forgive others. Forgiving oneself allows oneself to love unconditionally and have the confidence to let negativity go but we often stumble over this.

Letting go of "stuff" is a key component in forgiving...I've known many people in my lifetime who forgive but never "forget." I really believe that it's not truly forgiveness if you cannot forget.

If you keep bringing up the same ol' stuff and acting the same ol' way then you haven't released it all and you have not truly forgiven.

Hmmmm...

Let me say that again... If you keep bringing up the same ol' stuff and acting the same ol' way then you haven't released it all and you have not truly forgiven.

Should you let the person who hurt you travel in the same lane with you again? I'm not sure about that because you don't want to be stupid about it. You certainly can forgive and choose not to have that person in your life anymore or change the way they are in your life but harboring negative feelings is not reflective of forgiveness.

It all goes back to that old saying "What would Jesus do? Ask yourself "How many times has God forgiven me?"

Hmmmm…Begin to forgive folks.

Just plain ol' forgiveness.

LESSON:

> *Do you want to be forgiven?*

ACTION:

> *Think about who you can forgive today. Take one step to make that happen.*

Day 14

"He loves ME, She loves ME not..."

Some people love you the best way they know how...and then they give you the best that they have based on the best way they know how.

But for some of us that is not enough so we ask for more, require more and demand more. And then we are hurt and disappointed when we don't get it. But how can they give you more if they don't know more?

It then becomes your responsibility to determine what you will accept.

Will you lower your standards? Or, in some cases, *RAISE* your standards?

You have to know who you are to know what you want....And that person who doesn't love you in a "perfect" way may be loving you in the "only" way they know how, but it is up to YOU to decide if you want their love...

If it is the "right" type of love for you.

If it is truly the "best that they got" then you have to decide if it is the "best" that you will take. If their love is flawed, their commitment to that love suspicious, then it's your choice to remain in or to leave the relationship.

How do you want to be loved? How will you allow yourself to be loved?

Do you really want to be loved?

Remember, you are only treated the way you allow yourself to be treated and love cannot be trained because it is raw.

Nor is it transferable...you cannot substitute one love for another.

People will give you the love they have but you own the power to ask "Is it enough?"

You own the power of movement to walk away but you also have the choice to stay.

Yes, sometimes people love you the best way they know how but the way you love yourself determines if you will accept their love the best way you know how...

Hmmmm...

LESSON:

Self-love is the first true love...Don't depend on others to give it to you...They can't.

AFFIRMATION:

"I Love Me the best way I know how but when I know better, I will do better."

Day 15

"I can only be ME"

Letter to *YOU:*

> You see at the end of the day I will never
> stop being me.
> I will continue to live for me.
> Breathe for me.
> Work for me.
> Play for me.
> Believe in me. Die for me.
> Even if I don't make *YOU* happy.
> See, the tricky thing is that I really don't
> know how to be anything or anyone else
> but myself. And if you can't find your happy
> in that then we cannot co-exist in the same
> place.
> You see, I always know that "I am, I can, I
> will and I do."
> Despite of you.

It doesn't matter if you are my man, my woman, my mother, my father, sister, brother, boss or my friend...I am still only me and that's what you are going to get.

I am true to myself because I know that my strength lies within in.

That my spirit is full of the stuff that God made me with and that "no man" will take me under. My faith is the catalyst for the strengthening of the ivy vine that continuously connects me to my soul.

And my determination serves as the springboard that allows me to jump ahead of my own dreams.

There's no "ratchet-ness" over here because I am THAT beautiful woman who is "so much" and then again, she is "so much" more.

I have to think for myself to do for myself to love myself and to survive with myself.

My spiritual, emotional and psychological sobriety is just not dependent upon your responses and your requirements of me.

Nah, I can't go out like that.

I'm stronger than that because I really live for me and I know that God made me as I am because he believes in me.

Am I perfect? Hell naw!

And do I make lots of mistakes? Y'all already know I do.

But none of that stops me from being me. It's all I got.

And the end of the day when lights are off and it's just me, myself and I am laying in the bed, who am I going to talk to and get "real" answers besides God?

Yeah, that's right…it's only me.

So please, stop trying to change the way I think so you can change the way I behave…

I've got lots of dreams to fulfill and when one dream is done, I've got many others to go after so I'm empowered, uplifted and inspired…by my own self.

And, it feels good.

Damn good.

I got this.

So please just let me be me and take the time to go and discover your own self…You'll see the difference it will make in your world…

LESSON:

Always be yourself despite and in spite of what others try to make of you. Yes, sometimes you will have to "play the game" but never, ever forget that it's just a game and the real truth always comes out when you look into the mirror.

ACTION:

Think about the instances where you have to "play the game." Ask yourself "is it worth it?"

Day 16

"Don't Borrow Worries"

I know that there are some folks out there who disagree with my thoughts and my words. But that's okay because I don't answer to them.

And there are several, perhaps many, who just don't understand what I do and why I do it.

But that's okay too because I don't need their permission.

And yet there is still another group that remains "on the fence" just trying to figure me out...Not sure what to make of me.

But they can wobble all they want...They are not the shields of faith that I lead on.

You see I first look to my God to strengthen me and fill me up with the courage I'll need to get through.

And I look into the mirror each day to ensure that the reflection staring back at me is tenacious, innovative and sincere so we can stand strong together.

I've created my world of wonders with the people who are a part of it --- my selected family, my selected friends and positive-minded folks...

Since I've done this there really is no need to borrow worries and include those who are not believers.

You see, if we spend every waking hour trying to please others who really don't matter, and if we spend quality time responding to situations wrought with negativity, then when will we focus on our positive selves?

How can we follow our dreams if we spend so much time with our nightmares?

At what point do we *"Let Go and Let God?"*

When do we just "walk away" from the people and things that limit our possibilities?

And yes, we may have to walk down a long, sometimes lonely and uncomfortable road to get where we need to be but we already know that God has ordered our steps anyway.

Some folks just don't want what's right for you and they don't want you to get/receive what is rightfully yours.

They are the "blockers" in your life.

You have to figure how to get around these people who are blocking you from your blessings and your true self. Make your plan of escape.

Figure out how to remove that needle they used to pierce your life with fear and doubt...forcing negativity into your heart like a virus running through your bloodstream.

They must first be medicated and then removed like a cancerous tumor... But you have to be that surgeon for yourself.

At some point you've got to cleanse your own wounds so you can begin to heal and move forward....

Learn to doctor your own spirit by anesthetizing it with your faith, belief that you are a child of God and your self-empowerment...

There are always going to be that circle of people who don't believe in you, support your dreams or seek to do you harm....

But you just need to trust and believe in who you are and what you represent and their actions will begin not to matter in your life.

Remember, man doesn't determine your fate...the steps that God has ordered for you does... What's for you is already for you...You just have to claim it...

LESSON:

There are "haters" everywhere...Protect yourself with the love of God. After all, he's the only one that you really answer to.

AFFIRMATION:

"God orders my steps, not man."

Day 17

"I've Let Go already but now I have to Let God"

Some of us claim that we have adopted a *"Let Go and Let God"* philosophy to lead our lives but yet we want to "pick and choose" what we are going to "give" God to handle.

We often decide to only "allow" him to salvage the "messes" that we make and conquer any adversity that we may face.

We convince ourselves that we are people who are empowered and not enslaved so we are able-bodied and "strong" enough to handle what life has to offer so we don't share the battles with God until we feel we are losing the war.

You see, because we are self-confident some of our behaviors reek of arrogance...As though we know it all, been through it all and done it all at least two times.

We believe that our knowledge combined with our experience is the only guided tools we need to push us through the pain and make us feel good again.... So, we don't call on God until it hurts. And hurts real badly.

And then we realize that we can't do it alone...not by ourselves...we are now afraid and fear breeds confusion and doubt so we know that we need Jesus and we need him now so that's when decide to "Let Go and Let God."

Hmmmm....

What if we gave God the power and the glory for each and everything that we do daily?

Suppose we shared the emotional and psychological poverty with him from the beginning? Suppose we prayed that he would wrap his arms around us and hold us tight everyday so we are cloaked in his love and strength?

That his omnipotence would flow through us so we can feel his power in everything that we do....running through us like a nutrient in our bloodstreams?

What if we simply "believed" in the power of prayer and what God can and will do for us whether we like it or not?

See, I believe that God does have all the "extra" pieces we need to complete our life puzzles but we spend way too much time trying to figure it out ourselves...One piece at a time.

Yes, I am that "strong woman" and I think I can do it all but I know that I can do nothing, be nothing and achieve nothing with God's imprint on my life. He orders my steps and through triumph and tragedy he is the shield that I lean on....

When you *"Let Go and Let God"* you're letting him into your entire life....You are not simply "picking and choosing" because God is not a Choice. He is real and he is a Requirement to make it through daily....

To *"Let Go and Let God"* means "letting him in."

Let him into your decisions, your hopes, your dreams, your goals, your success and your failure...He'll enjoy being there because he loves you....Anyway.

Despite and in spite of everything else...

Yes. "Let Loose" so you can *"Let Go and Let God...."*

LESSON:

He sees what you are doing anyway so why not send him your personal invitation to share your life with him?

ACTION:

Write down 3 ways in the past month that you have "Let Go and Let God." Ask yourself: "What difference has it made in my life?"

Day 18

"I'm not afraid"

Fear not what you need the most.

Fear not what you want the least.

Sometimes we become afraid of our own dreams

And stagnate our steps to make them a reality.

We create barriers to our own success by what we

do and what we fail to do.

We put protective armor around our souls in an

effort to shield our hearts from pain

And our spirits from being broken

But know that as long as you believe that God

orders your steps then your dreams can never

become your nightmares.

Be prepared that when God says "Yes!" he may

take you to places you've never been...

You may travel roads that are not paved and you

may climb mountains yet unnamed.

Those valleys that you stumble upon may cause you to fall down a few times but remember that this is the path that He has chosen for you.

And he has never failed you yet.

Fear of the unknown should not detour you from following your dreams. It's what you do already know that will most likely be your alternate route away from greatness.

Your emotional and spiritual sobriety should not be dependent on warped ideas.

But instead should rely on the faith of God's plans for you....

Fear not.

Be not.

Give up not.

Your steps have already been ordered.

What's for you is already for you.

Just be prepared and begin the journey and fear not yourself.

LESSON:

Sometimes we are afraid to dream because we are afraid to fail and we don't clearly understand our destiny. But when God calls you to "do you," be not afraid because he's "got your back." Go for it. Take a chance. Live being who you really are, who God has chosen you to be...That means following those dreams and walking down that uncomfortable road of the unknown. Fear not because God is always by your side.

AFFIRMATION:

"I am not afraid and I got this 'cuz my God has me..."

Day 19

"To Forgive or To Forget?"

Apologies are often more difficult to accept than if we had to relive the event that caused the hurt in the first place.

This is extremely hard to do if when you feel as though you have given all that you can and people seem to hurt you anyway.

How do you know or how can you forgive those who inflicted pain in your life?

Yes, it's hard but we have to do it.

We do it to move forward and to begin the next phase of our lives.

If we spend our time harboring negative feelings and "holding on" to old hurt then we does the true healing process begin?

When will we allow ourselves to be happy again?

I realized long ago that if I rejected an apology and held on to my anger then I would be holding on to negativity and that would chip away at the positive energy in my life.

That's the energy that allows me to love.

If I forgive someone then I can move forward and they no longer take up emotional, psychological and physical space in my life.

I've been hurt sooooooo many times in my life by friends, acquaintances, colleagues and family but I've learned to accept apologies and move on...

Holding on to hurtful situations will only impregnate me with more heartache and pain and I will only protect that hurt with anger and negativity.

Walking that long, uncomfortable road of forgiveness is not easy but it is necessary and required to be a true "Christian."

We have demands of us if we accept that title and forgiveness is one of them. It is the "heart" of what it means to be a "Christian."

And that also means forgiving yourself which is sometimes the hardest thing to do.

Sometimes we can't figure out how to do that so we turn to God and ask for forgiveness …

We do it again and again…

How many times have we prayed for forgiveness? Lost count right?

We think that if God can forgive us then that will empower us to forgive ourselves. If we struggle with forgiving ourselves then how can we know how to forgive others?

Hmmmm…

Begin your process of healing by apologizing to yourself first…

Free yourself from that jail of hurt that you have sentenced yourself to.

Liberate your emotional enslavement to your mistakes of the past and write your own proclamation of freedom from barbed wired surrounding your heart and soul.

You need to do this first so you can begin accepting apologies, forgiving and forgetting others…. Simply put, "get over it, get through it and keep it moving."

Yes, accepting apologies can be soooooo difficult for us….

Sometimes it's just easier to be angry and hurt because we feel like we're in control…

Like we have the power because the other person owes us that apology and it's up to us to accept it.

We want them to hurt like they hurt us so we use the rejection of an apology as a weapon of emotional destruction….

Hmmmm…

Is it worth it?

Forgiving others is a challenge but we can do it because we are supposed to.

We have requirements to be a true "Christian" and expectations as human beings…

Just know that just because you forgive someone doesn't mean that you have to allow them back in your life…

Actually it is "freeing" yourself from the imprisonment of your feelings...you can let all of those negative feelings go as you let that person go out of your life... Just think about it...

LESSON:

If you want forgiveness, learn how to forgive.

ACTION:

List 1 thing that you need to forgive yourself for. List 2 things that you need to forgive others for.

Day 20

"My New Normal"

*Letter to **YOU:***

What is your "new normal?"

Is it that you now have confidence in
yourself to believe that your dreams are
destined to come true?

That it's okay to never, ever stop dreaming?

That when one dream has been fulfilled you
should start working on the next one?

Is it that you no longer limit your
possibilities?

Or allow any disabilities to disable your
abilities?

Or could it be that your life now includes
prayers that thank your heavenly Father?

That you now understand that if faith can

move mountains it will surely have no
problem moving you too?

What is your "new normal?"
Can it be that you now accept that just
because you may experience economic
poverty you are not emotionally, spiritually
or intellectually impoverished?

Is it that you have learned that some people
love you the best way they know how but it
is up to you to decide if that love will be
enough?
That not everyone is your friend?
Or, that everyone is not your enemy either?
And you now love yourself first before
giving it all the love away to everyone else?

What is your "new normal?"
Does this mean that you know now that
living for today is not so bad after all?
And that you shouldn't "borrow worries"

because they are nonrefundable and cannot be exchanged? Besides, nobody wants them back anyway?

What about forgiveness? Have you now forgiven yourself so you can move forward? Or, have you learned that you own the power of change but it is worthless if you don't use it?

Have you made the changes in your life that restrain you from achieving your greatness? That life really is about what you make it…the good and the bad…It's all about how you perceive what is happening around you….

That triumph and challenge is about "mind over matter." As much as you "mind" will be as much as it "matters." And if you don't "mind," then it really shouldn't "matter?"

Your "new normal" should be about your new approach to your life and how you nurture it, strengthen it and empower it. It may take you down uncomfortable roads that lead to the path of greatness and it should remind you that God has already ordered your steps so you are going to be okay.

Yes, your "new normal" should give you a piece of mind, a settled spirit and a rejuvenated soul...Pretty soon it won't feel so "new" anymore and will just a "normal" part of you...

What things are your "new normal?"

LESSON:

The power of positive thinking...The strengthening of the mind to empower the soul--- The "New Normal."

AFFIRMATION:

"My NEW Normal is actually quite normal now..."

Day 21

"I am not ashamed..."

Letter to *YOU:*

There have been some things in my life that I
probably should have just walked away from.

Certain situations, certain people and certain
things
But I made that conscientious decision to stay.

Stay to fight for it.
Stay to believe in it.
Stay to trust in it.
And stay because I just felt "I needed to."

I really didn't look at it as right or wrong...
It was what it was and I did what I had to do.
I did what I knew best and when I knew better
I did better.

That's the power of resiliency.

We lean on our shields of hope to help us get through tough times

And we rely on our hearts to guide us in the right direction.

But what about our faith?

At what point are do we open the windows of our souls to allow faith to breeze into our lives?

When do we give credit to the sweet spirit of God performing his miracles in our lives?

For understanding that it was God's will the entire time that permitted us to stay in situations, things and with some people that everyone else thought we should have given up on?

Now don't get me wrong...I'm not saying that it was God's grace that authorized abuse in your life or the Devil's work on your daily existence.

But it has been through the steps that he has ordered for you that you found the audacity of hope, dreams and the tenacity cloaked by courage to keep fighting for what you believed in.

Sometimes it's God's whisper that has the loudest voice around us and we must be still to hear it.

We must silence all anguish, doubt, fear, shame, confusion, sadness, frustration, denial, despair and negative attitudes to hear the voice of God speaking directly to us.

Silence people and things around you and you will feel God's direct message to you.

So when I tell you that I stood firm in certain situations, things and with certain people I am saying this because I heard my God's words speaking to me.

I felt his presence in my decisions because I consulted him.

I asked for his guidance and asked for him to wrap his arms around me and hold me tight as I made difficult choices in my life.

To nourish my starving and confused heart and mind with the nutrients of obedience, self-love and self-empowerment so I could believe in my choices and know that failure has never been an option in my life.

And were my decisions always right?

Hmmmm...

I am a happy, healthy and spirit-filled woman right now, today, at this very moment so I would say *YES!*

Were my decisions "easy" to live with just because I had God on my side?

NO!

But it was easier to live with myself knowing I made my choice with God on my side.

You see, it's all about faith for me.

All about remembering that if faith the size of a mustard seed can move a big ol' mountain then it would have no problem moving me too.

I trust.

I believe.

And know that at the end of the day when it is only me lying in the bed with my thoughts that I know I have to love me and live the rest of my life with any decisions that I've made...

But I can do it because the windows to my soul are always open and the breezes of God and faith are always blowing in my direction.

And, it feels good. Damn good.

LESSON: Breezes are always blowing...whether you open your windows or not. Choose to leave

them open... "Fresh" air can be soooo good for you.

ACTION: Reflect on 2 challenging decisions that you had to make in your life...How do you feel about them now?

Day 22

"Don't SAVE it, USE it!"

I know we've all heard folks say "I'm saving the BEST for LAST."

Hmmmm...

If they do that then what the hell are they giving me right now?

Raise your hand if you want folks to give you their "half-ass" best at any time.

Didn't think so.

So why do we do it to ourselves?

Why do we give our best to others and try to "save the best for last" for ourselves?

The problem is that by the time we get to ourselves there is usually nothing left or just a little bit leftover.

And then we wonder why we are dissatisfied and can't reach our goals in love, happiness and success.

You see, you need to remember that you are "the best" and so you only deserve "the best."

Not just from others but from yourself first.

You've got gifts. Share them with yourself first.

You've got talents. Cultivate them with yourself first.

You've got skills. Train them for yourself first.

You've got faith. Believe in it for yourself first.

You've got God. Listen to him for yourself first. Yes, it's okay to "do you" first...to give yourself wholly and freely to you first in order to be happy...That's how it's supposed to be.

If you can't please yourself first then how will you know how to please others?

If you can't give yourself the "best" then how do you really know what your "best" looks like? Hmmmm...

"Save the best for last" just doesn't work when you are trying to put your best foot forward first. You will end up in the "last place" in line for success if you keep giving away all of your "good stuff."

LESSON:

If you don't give your best to you don't expect anyone to do it FOR you...it just doesn't work that way. Self-Love, Self-Respect and Self-Empowerment all begin with the SELF first! It's okay...You can share with the world after you get it together with yourself first.

AFFIRMATION:

"It's ME FIRST today!"

Day 23

"I OWN my dreams"

The bottom line is that you are responsible for your own dreams...

You cannot expect anyone else to make your dreams a reality for you. You have to create your dream and work your dream to live your dream...That's your responsibility so don't expect others to do it for you.

The one thing that I have learned throughout my life experience is that the more you depend on others will be the more that you will learn to depend on yourself because folks just won't get it done for you.

But why should they?

Is it their dream? Is it their investment?

Folks can support you to infinity and beyond with their love and positive thoughts but don't wait on them to do things for you...They mean well but they have their own dreams to fulfill so you can't expect them to work on yours.

Sad, but it is ultimately true.

You are the only one who can make your dreams become a reality for you so begin to create your plan of action.

When developing your path to your destiny you should include those things that are "perfect" so you can always see what you are trying to achieve but also include the "worst possible scenario" so that you are well aware of what could go wrong. Know that the path you take could be the road less travelled but that's okay because that only means that there is more room for you to navigate on the road to greatness.

Know that your path may be full of pebbles and rocks but those are only the stepping stones you have to climb to achieve your dream.

And know that it may not be "easy" but it is "easiest" if you remain positive and grounded.

You may hear a lot of words such as be "No, Maybe and I'll See" before you finally hear that "Yes" but that's just a part of the movement...

Be prepared for the work...get your mind right and know that this is what you really want to do because at the end of the day it is your dream that you are following and you are responsible for it.

Some folks may interpret your confidence as self-arrogance and others will view you as a "pillar of strength" as you struggle for your significance in your dream.

Be prepared for that as well but know that you are on a mission to work that dream to live that dream...despite and in spite of others.

It's okay to question yourself, check yourself and change yourself along the way but never lose sight of who you really are...

You may have to "play some games" to get where you want/need to be but know that these are just games you are playing and remember who you really are under it all...

So, I've said this before but it is appropriate again...

What happens to a dream deferred?

Nothing. Absolutely nothing.

Don't let it happen. Period.

Your dreams are your responsibility...they don't belong to anyone else so don't give them away...Nurture and nurse those dreams as though you gave physical birth to them...Treat them as though they are your children...Most folks do not give their children up for adoption so don't give your dreams away either. Love them. Respect them and work for them so that they ultimately remain positive dreams and not scary nightmares...

Ahhh yes, those dreams are real and the responsibility is really yours...Take the responsibility and make it a reality.

LESSON:

The Dream is Real. Work it to Live it.

ACTION:

List your top 2 dreams today. List one action you took to make that dream a reality in the past week.

Day 24

"I Love ME some ME!"

There's something about loving yourself that makes you feel whole.

There's something about trusting yourself that makes you feel honest.

There's something about believing in yourself that makes you feel that dreams can come true.

And there's something about thanking God for creating you just as you are that makes you feel special.

So why do always forget these things?

See sometimes we don't embrace how beautiful we are, how smart we are and we focus on the things we are not.

We don't think about all the good we have done but can quickly write a list of all the wrong we've a part of.

And we don't remember that we are important and we deserve more because we have trained ourselves to settle for less.

Why is it so hard for us to be good to ourselves?

We wrap our hearts around other people first and then we try to love ourselves with whatever is left.

But that's not enough.

Our souls need more to give more.

Our spirits require more to share more.

And our emotional well-being thrives on positivity to become more.

But if we always neglect who we are to focus on what we think we should be then how do we appreciate the person who we live with today?

I know we all strive to accomplish things in our lives but sometimes we just need to be STILL.

We need to listen to the voices within.

And feel the strength of our inner selves... We can love ourselves stronger this way.

And know that we really are independent, free-spirited, priceless and honest...Enough to love ourselves to "infinity and beyond."

When was the last time that you looked in the mirror and said "I Love You!"?

Hmmmm...

But yet we tell others every day.

And we show them in so many ways.

You see if we don't love ourselves, affirm ourselves and commit to ourselves then how do we empower ourselves?

If we don't pay more attention to ourselves and to who we really are then at some point when we look into that mirror again we will be staring at an empty reflection...at a person that never really was.

Yeah, there's just something about lovin' yourself that makes you stronger...And makes you happy to be you so much longer...

LESSON:

Don't forget to love on yourself first...You have to love you, trust you, believe in you and empower you before you are any good to anyone else.

AFFIRMATION:

"I LOVE Me Some ME!"

Day 25

"Bootstraps of Faith"

You have to go hard to live hard and to live right...That's the only way to live a prosperous life. For me, that's the only way I know how to move beyond hurtful places. I go hard so I don't have to hurt hard and I have been successful because of this drive. I now that you must first change the way you think before you can change the way you behave. I think that you have it within yourself to make positive changes as well.

A few years ago an acquaintance said that she was tired of hearing that people should "pull themselves up by their bootstraps to be successful." Her concern was "what if folks don't have any bootstraps at all to pull themselves up from?" She was making the point that some people have nothing and therefore can't see a better tomorrow because they are stuck in "yesterdays" and barely functioning today.

Hmmmm...

I don't agree with her thoughts and I don't think you should either. I think that NOT having bootstraps is actually impossible as long as you have *FAITH*. If *FAITH* is strong enough to move mountains it is definitely stronger to move you towards positive change too. I don't think that my God has put anyone here on this earth without the ability to have *FAITH* in *His* creations. For some it is more challenging and they may hear more "no's" than "yes's" in their lives but I think that if you hold on to your bootstrap of *FAITH* then you know that "your time" is coming.

Everyone's story is different but we all need to thrive on the *FAITH* that has been God-given and use this faith as a bootstrap to pull oneself out of any pits of despair, disappointment and disenfranchisement. Just because you may have been born into economic poverty does not mean that you have to be spiritually, emotionally, psychologically and intellectually impoverished as well.

My own life story tells the tale of how I used my own bootstraps to pull me up, how I used those same bootstraps to bring volume to my silenced voice and how I hung on to those bootstraps when I stumbled on many occasions.

My life history reflects resiliency and triumph through adversity because I learned long ago that there are 6 ways that know what we know about life --- tradition, personal experience, intuition, logic, expert opinion and research. To reach my current level of functioning I focus on the first four ways of knowing...they have been the cornerstone of my existence and have made a difference in the choices I've made in my life. These have been some of the bootstraps I use to pull me up out of any despair, negativity, hopelessness so that I could rise up and claim all victories that were mine!

You can do it too! Find your bootstraps and dust them off! Hang on to your FAITH and you will also move toward positive change in your own life. Remember, no one has ever bathed in your water, danced in your shoes to the same beat, sat in your chair at the same time or walked on your personal path so they cannot GIVE you *FAITH*...you have believe in it for yourself....

LESSON:

FAITH is alive.

ACTION:

List 3 things that can serve as your bootstraps to help you lift yourself out of any pits of despair, disappointment and disenfranchisement.

Day 26

"My Faith Moves My Mountains"

It's funny how just when we think we are "over" something or someone it only takes one instance to remind us that we are not.

When your heart is broken there is not a surgery that can piece it back together to its original form. There will always be the stitches to show how it was repaired and then the scar to remind you of the wound.

And the time it takes to heal is never known because each hurt is so different and the depth and breadth of the hurt changes with each situation.

It's scary to think that you are "over it" and then you realize that it still hurts.

So what can you do?

Hmmmm...Probably not much at all.

Buttttt....We can always try.

We don't always own the power of love and pain.

We can't help who we love and we can only limit our pain but we are going to feel.

That's what makes us uniquely human.

And we when we feel sometimes that brings us pain.

But we can lean on our shields of faith and know that tomorrow is just a day away.

That after the rain the sun eventually comes out.

That after the winter the spring always comes.

That after the complex twists and turns in the road there will be a straight-away coming up, that after dipping deep in the valley of despair we will start climbing up the hills and mountains to reach our happy places.

That after the labor pains there is a birth that will remind us of the wonder of life.

That after teaching there is a lesson learned.

That after hard work there is always time to play and that after we have drained our minds/bodies of self-made positivity then our faith is there to replenish us.

So you see, although there are some things that we may NEVER get over in our lives we can still get through them.

While we can't necessarily control who we love or when we hurt we can control the effect it can have on our lives.

Having faith helps us to know that the hurt will soon be filled with the happy and the pain will be swapped out for pleasure.

Faith does that for you.

Yes, hurt hurts.

And we want it to go away.

I absolutely hate it when it comes back...that "surprise bumping-into" meeting, the old photo that you come across, a song you hear and simple birthday that you remember can stir those emotions that cause you to hurt.

You just never know what will trigger these feelings... But what you can hold on to is that your faith will pull you through it all.

I've said this many times and I'm going to say it again here....

Faith is a miraculous healer... It's a "mover" and a "shaker."

If faith the size of a mustard seed can move mountains then it can surely move you...

Know it.

Keep it.

Empower and embrace yourself in it.

Love yourself for believing in it.

LESSON:

You can't always control your pain but you can always have faith that you will get through it.

AFFIRMATION:

"My faith is stronger than my pain."

Day 27

"Too Damn Picky"

Some of us claim that we have adopted a *"Let Go and Let God"* philosophy to lead our lives but yet we want to "pick and choose" what we are going to "give" God to handle.

We often decide to only "allow" him to salvage the "messes" that we make and conquer any adversity that we may face.

We convince ourselves that we are people who are empowered and not enslaved so we are able-bodied and "strong" enough to handle what life has to offer so we don't share the battles with God until we feel we are losing the war.

You see, because we are self-confident some of our behaviors reek of arrogance...

As though we know it all, been through it all and done it all at least two times.

We believe that our knowledge combined with our experience, are the only guided tools we need to push us through the pain and make us feel good again....

So, we don't call on God until it hurts.

And hurts real badly.

And we realize that we can't do it alone...not by ourselves...we are now afraid and fear breeds confusion and doubt so we know that we need Jesus and we need him now so that's when decide to *"Let Go and Let God."*

Hmmmm...

What if we gave God the power and the glory for each and everything that we do daily?

Suppose we shared the emotional and psychological poverty with him from the beginning? Suppose we prayed that he would wrap his arms around us and hold us tight everyday so we are cloaked in his love and strength?

That his omnipotence would flow through us so we can feel his power in everything that we do....running through us like a nutrient in our bloodstreams?

What if we simply "believed" in the power of prayer and what God can and will do for us whether we like it or not?

See, I believe that God does have all the "extra" pieces we need to complete our life puzzles but we spend way too much time trying to figure it out ourselves...One piece at a time.

Yes, I am that "strong woman" and I think I can do it all but I know that I can do nothing, be nothing and achieve nothing without God's imprint on my life.

He orders my steps and through triumph and tragedy he is the shield that I lean on....

When you *"Let Go and Let God"* you're letting him into your entire life....

You are not simply "picking and choosing" because God is not a Choice.

He is real and he is a Requirement to make it through daily....

To *"Let Go and Let God"* means "letting him in."

Let him into your decisions, your hopes, your dreams, your goals, your success and your failure... He'll enjoy being there because he loves you....

Anyway.

Despite and In spite of everything.

LESSON:

Trust and believe so that so you can "Let Go and Let God...." He knows what you are doing anyway so why not?

ACTION:

List 3 things that you know you really should "Let Go and Let God" handle.

Day 28

"Get Out of My Life! Just GO!"

Have you ever tried to let go of somebody?

To remove them from your life?

You know that it's really what you're supposed to

do, should do, and need to do but not sure how to

do it or if you even really want to but you

understand you have to.

It's so hard...

When you love hard, you also hurt hard.

I've learned that as long as it took for you to learn

how to love the person it will take at least double

that amount of time to let them go out of your life.

You didn't love them overnight so you won't be

able to let them go overnight either.

You see, it's "double duty" now because you are

trying to train yourself to not love them anymore

and to not let them be a part of your daily life.

So yes, letting them go hurts so bad.

You want to call but you don't.

You want to text but you won't.

And you want to stop thinking about them but you can't....

The thought of them invades your dreams and the memories of the good times together may start to trick you into thinking that perhaps you made a mistake in letting them go out of your life.

But your heart knows the truth and it knows how bad this person made you feel countless times.

Your spirit remembers how bruised it was when they lost faith in you.

And your soul still feels the holes left behind when this person shot the bullets of negativity through it.

So you already know that they have to go...

They can no longer rent space in your heart, spirit, soul and your life.

But it's so damn hard to let them go.

Love of others runs deep.

But the love of you should run deeper.

Love yourself more than the hurt.

Love yourself more than that person.

Love yourself as God loves you...To infinity and beyond.

Learn that at the end of the day it's just you staring at yourself in the mirror...

Can you stand the sight of yourself if you remain in that relationship?

You must learn to let go of ANY type of relationship--family, friends, coworkers, boyfriends, girlfriends, bad habits, etc.

And know that it will be hard...It's supposed to be....

When you are fighting for your heart, spirit and soul you will receive some battle wounds and perhaps some scars too.

But that doesn't mean that you have to reject the surgery and allow them back into your life...

Instead be prepared to "suit up" in your armor to fight for your heart, spirit and soul...

Wake up every day with your prayers for strength

and just take it one move at a time.

Don't text him.

"Decline" her phone call.

"Trash" their inbox messages.

Force yourself to think of your favorite foods when you begin to think about him/her....Shift your mindset.

Yes, letting go of someone from your life is a process

But it is definitely one worth going through.

LESSON:

It takes time to let go but months from now you'll look back and know that you made the right choice when you look into the mirror and can smile at that person looking back at you.

AFFIRMATION:

"I'm worth releasing all people and things that are not worthy of me."

Day 29

"Divorced and Happy"

Who is your pain married to?

Who does it recite vows of commitment to everyday?

What is your hurt assigned to protect?

That forces you to wear shields of armor and bulletproof vests against those who want to help you through the hurt?

And what type of long-term contract have you signed with anguish and bad habits in your life?

Why don't you want to get through it?

What makes you stay wallowing in the despair?

Where is your safe haven? The place you feel whole?

Sometimes we hold on to the pain so long that it just becomes a part of our daily lives.

And then we can't tell the difference between our joy and our pain because our emotions have become so numb.

We claim hopelessness when we fall out of love because we think that we will never love again.

We claim forgetfulness when we should be happy because we don't remember what it feels like to feel good.

And we accept "second-handness" in some of our relationships because we think that we don't deserve "the best" in our lives so we accept the "sloppy seconds."

Our emotional and mental sobriety becomes dependent on the level of hurt and pain that we may feel on any given day.

And that pain can come from anywhere but will marry your soul and you won't know how to let it go...how to divorce the emptiness, the heartache and misery from our lives.

This is more than a "marriage of convenience"...It is symbolic of a union of negativity, desolation, sadness, distress and grief.

And the only way to free yourself is to believe in the power of change.

Believe that you must first change the way you think in order to change the way you behave.

Believe that life can change if you want it...if you allow it and if you take the steps to make it happen.

Pain does not change by itself...You have to use your spirit of positivity as the key to unlock your jail of loneliness because you really are not alone...unless you want to be.

Draft those separation papers first to begin the process of removing yourself from everything and everyone who continue to hurt you.

Sign the legal documents that will enable you to release the self-inflicting toxins that you have been inhaling.

See the judge for the final decree of divorce for all the old heartache and pain that you have suffered over the years but have been unable to let go.

You don't want any of it anymore...you don't need any of it anymore and you don't have to have any of it anymore...

Get over it. Get through it. And keep it moving. Sometimes we need that divorce...we need to "un-marry" ourselves from the negative energy in our lives...

We need to understand that we are not "special" in our lives because we've been "through" stuff and it hurts. And we don't get a "pass" just because it happened to us...

We own the power of change so we need to use that power in our own lives...

Get over it. Get through it. And keep it moving. Cancel that subscription. Block that number and file those papers today.

LESSON:

Sometimes Divorce is the only option.

ACTION:

*List 3 things you need to divorce yourself from and
3 things that you need to be married to.*

Day 30

"Let Them Go!"

If someone is in your life that pulls while you push,

Let them go.

If someone is in your life that makes you feel bad

just so they can feel good,

Let them go.

If there is someone walking around in your world

that puts salt in your sugar,

Then you just don't need them in your life.

Although you may not be able to choose who you

love because it's such a raw and natural emotion

you do own the power to choose what you do with

that love and who you allow in your life.

You see, our lives our full of good and bad

relationships but at some point we need to discern

between the two.

At some point we need clarity about which

relationships work for us and which people are just

toxins in our lives.

Who are these folks who poison us with their words and venomous actions?

And it's not all about thinking and feeling selfishly...

It's just about looking out for self.

Protecting oneself.

Rebuilding oneself.

Recreating oneself.

Improving oneself.

Reclaiming oneself.

You see if we remain caught up in a situation that breeds negativity we will only continue to give birth to hurt and pain that is cloaked in a blanket of shame and doubt.

We will never reach a level of positivity.

If we always bathe in our own dirt of despair and fail to lean on our shields of faith for our support then we will always embrace a source of false Herculean strength.

And then we can only just hope that this will be enough to get us through.

But it won't because it never did.

And it never will.

We have to be willing to just give it up to get over it, get through it and keep it moving.

If they can't be there *FOR* you then are they really in your life *WITH* you?

If they cannot say "AMEN" after your prayer then were they even praying at all?

And if you have to question their purpose, integrity and commitment to your excellence do you really need them in your life?

Yes, we all need support to help us become who we dream of becoming, accomplish what we planned to do and claim the victories that belong to us.

But we don't have to allow ourselves to be psychologically, emotionally and spiritually assassinated to receive that support.

Let them go.

Give it up.

Get Over It!

LESSON:

Sometimes we search too hard outside of our "circles" for the things that can hurt us but we must also remember that to turn ourselves "inside out" because we may find the real source of our pain already sharing the same space with us. If someone is in your life that is pulling while you are pushing, let them go!

AFFIRMATION:

"Today I will turn myself inside out to find out what's hurting me."

Day 31

"Make That Change"

Sometimes changing the way you think is just so damn hard.

Your heart wants to but your mind plays tricks on you and makes you believe that you can't.

When you want to be "out" of love with someone because it's "just time" and you feel like you are loving them longer and harder you feel so weak.

And when you want to change that job because it just doesn't meet your needs anymore you feel so scared of what the future may bring.

And changing the way you think about certain situations so you can maintain relationships and "peace" in your life seems like a daunting task.

So you second guess yourself.

You want to do the right thing so you pray for guidance.

You want to feel the right thing so you pray for inspiration.

But yet, it is just so damn hard.

See changing the way we think requires a shift in our ideological, philosophical, spiritual and emotional paradigms.

Ideological, philosophical, spiritual and emotional paralysis can have a worst impact than physical paralysis. If you don't feel anything in your heart and your soul and you don't use your brain then you have paralyzed your ability to live a happy life...you can live a fulfilled life with a physical paralysis but I'm not convinced that you can do it if you are living with a spiritual paralysis.

It demands that we acknowledge our greatest strengths may also be our greatest weaknesses.

And it requires our resiliency in the raw.

We have to reject failure as an option.

And embrace success as the only solution.

We need to want the mindset change so badly that we are willing to change our lifestyle and our "life-beings" because of it.

We have to remove the layers of fear, anguish, despair, doubt, shame and "fakeness" to begin to change our minds to live healthier lifestyles. This is all the stuff our change gets caught up in.

Remember that just like that bucket of water that can be eventually filled with one drop at a time, your mindset can shift with one thought at a time... Healthy minds lead to healthy behavior which takes us down the path to a healthy life.

Is it hard? Uhhh, YEAH!

It is easier to live in that comfortable hell than to strive for existence in an uncomfortable heaven so we settle to remain in the mindset that we've always had.

We are so afraid...we have that fear of the unknown and that "drama-free" zone that we don't allow ourselves to grow and become what we are destined to be. But dreams don't come with a warranty or guarantee so we need to change our thought process to achieve them.

There is no "master" plan to change our minds

....We simply begin by recognizing that the change has to begin from within...

But change can hurt so bad that we just don't want to do it even though we already know that we own the power of change so we must exercise that power and begin with ourselves...

If you change the way you think, you will change the way you behave....If you change the way you behave then you will change the way you live....

And I know it takes courage...but I also know that we are all born with courage but it's when we use it at the right time that makes us courageous. Changing our minds is the first step in that process....

LESSON:

Change happens with one movement at a time.

ACTION:

Think about the things in your life that you can change your mind about today. Think about the things in your life that you can actually change today. Now DO it today.

"Just Another Day"

Some days I wake up and I just want to be

so much more...

I want to dream more, love more and feel

more.

I want to give more, accept more and do

more.

I want to dig into my soul more.

I want to pray more.

I want to be successful more.

I want to be independent more.

I want to be rich more.

I want to learn more.

I want to be confident more.

I want to be courageous more.

I want to be healthy more.

I want to be happy more.

I want to be funny more.

I want to smile more and laugh more.

I even want to be cute more.

And I want to believe in me more.

But most of all I want to be thankful and faithful more.

I deserve all of this....And More.

LESSON:

There is always "more" but sometimes you are already the "most" because God created you just as you are. Begin to ask yourself "why" you need "more" of anything...That may tell you what you have "less" of...

"I WILL BE HAPPY!"

ABOUT THE AUTHOR

Dr. White-johnson is the author of *"Go Hard and Stumble Softly"* published in July, 2012. She is also the author of *"Get Over It! How to Bounce Back after Hitting Rock Bottom"* and *"Get Over It! How to Bounce Back after Hitting Rock Bottom for Teens."* In addition, she has created a leadership and personal development program for teens that is aligned with the national Common Core Standards and the American School Counselor Association National Model Standards. She earned her Ph.D. from the University at Buffalo and holds a master's degree in the counseling field. Dr. White-johnson is married and the mother of five children.